DEAR MOTHER

1979

Dear Mom,
Merry Christmas with love
Bill, Greta, Bill + Jim

Dear Mother

Beautiful Writings
Of Praise, Love and Gratitude

Selected by Kitty Clevenger

Hallmark Editions

The publisher wishes to thank those who have given their kind permission to re-
print material included in this book. Every effort has been made to give proper
acknowledgments. Any omissions or errors are deeply regretted, and the publisher,
upon notification, will be pleased to make necessary corrections in subsequent
editions.

ACKNOWLEDGMENTS: "Definition" from *Poems of Inspiration and Courage* by
Grace Noll Crowell. Copyright 1936 by Harper & Row, Publishers, Inc.; renewed
1964 by Grace Noll Crowell. Reprinted by permission of the publisher. Excerpt
from *The Art of Living* by André Maurois. Reprinted by permission of Gerald
Maurois, Executor of the Estate of André Maurois. "A Mother" by Norman Vin-
cent Peale. Reprinted by permission of the author. "What Is a Mother?" from *What
Is a Mother*, edited by Lee Parr McGrath and Joan Scobey. Published by Essandess
Special Editions, a Division of Simon & Schuster, Inc. Copyright 1968 by Lee Parr
McGrath and Joan Scobey. Reprinted by permission of the publisher. "Mother is a
gardener..." by J. Harold Gwynne. ©J. Harold Gwynne. "Young Mother" by Kay
Wissinger from *The Chicago Tribune*. Reprinted by permission of *The Chicago
Tribune* and the author.

A mother is all those wonderful things
you never outgrow
your need for.

Kay Andrew

$\mathcal{G}$entle is a mother's love.

Ed Cunningham

THIS IS A MOTHER

This is a mother —
Warmth and tenderness
And soft dresses
That smell of sunshine,
Songs and stories
And smiling eyes
That say, "I love you,"
Gentle hands
That can comfort a kitten
Or shape a sugar cookie
Or lift a little one
Close, close, close to her heart
To a lovely world
Of trust and security.
A mother personifies
Shared understanding —
Confident faith —
Unalterable love.
This is a mother.

Doris Chalma Brock

SPRINGTIME

The seasons come
    And the seasons go
    And many the changes they bring,
But in the warmth
    Of a mother's heart,
    It is forever spring.

Barbara Burrow

Though distance may come
    between a mother and her child,
the bond that holds them close will never weaken —
    the love they share
    will never be more than a memory apart.

Dean Walley

A MOTHER'S PICTURE

A lady, the loveliest
   ever the sun looked down upon,
You must paint for me.
O, if I could only make you see
The clear blue eyes, the tender smile,
The sovereign sweetness, the gentle grace,
The woman's soul, and the angel's face,
That are beaming on me all the while,
But I need not speak these foolish words;
   One word tells you all I would say,
She is my mother; and you will agree
   That all the rest may be thrown away.

Alice Cary

HER LITTLE SHADOWS

I saw a young mother
With eyes full of laughter,
And two little shadows
Came following after.
Wherever she moved,
They were always right there —
Holding on to her skirts,
Hanging on to her chair,
Before her, behind her —
An adhesive pair.

"Don't you ever get weary
As day after day
Your two little tagalongs
Get in your way?"

She smiled as she shook
Her pretty young head,
And I'll always remember
The words that she said:

"It's good to have shadows
  That run when you run,
  That laugh when you're happy
  And hum when you hum —
  For you only have shadows
  When your life's filled with sun!"

Martha Wadsworth

TRANSFORMATION

Mighty is the force of motherhood! It trans-
forms all things by its vital heat; it turns
timidity into fierce courage, and dreadless de-
fiance into tremulous submission; it turns
thoughtlessness into foresight, and yet stills
all anxiety into calm content; it makes selfishness become self-denial, and gives even to
hard vanity the glance of admiring love.

George Eliot

FLOWERS FOR MOTHER

These velvet roses
   fringed with Queen Anne's Lace,
Do they recall my first bouquet to you?
That ragged bunch of wilted dandelions
You treasured and arranged in your best vase?

The broken stems, the accidental weeds
I brought when I was small,
   received the care
Of lavish blooms in later years. It's true
A mother's love is all a flower needs.

Georgia Sykes Sullivan

When God thought of mother, He must have
laughed with satisfaction and framed it quickly
— so rich, so deep, so divine, so full of soul,
power and beauty was the conception.

Henry Ward Beecher

A MOTHER'S LOVE

A mother's love! What can compare with it! Of all things on earth, it comes nearest to divine love in heaven.

A mother's love means a life's devotion — and sometimes a life's sacrifice — with but one thought, one hope and one feeling, that her children will grow up healthy and strong, free from evil habits and able to provide for themselves. Her sole wish is that they may do their part like men and women, avoid dangers and pitfalls, and when dark hours come, trust in Providence to give them strength, patience and courage to bear up bravely.

Happy is the mother when her heart's wish is answered, and happy are her sons and daughters when they can feel that they have contributed to her noble purpose and, in some measure, repaid her unceasing, unwavering love and devotion.

Author Unknown

A mother is the best friend
anyone ever has.

Author Unknown

A SPECIAL NEED

Sometimes you need someone
   who'll listen,
Sometimes you need someone
   who'll smile,
Sometimes you need someone
   who cares about you
   to just be around for a while.
Sometimes you need someone
   who'll help you,
Sometimes you need someone
   who'll share,
And those are the times
   when you can depend
   on a mother to always be there.

Karen Ravn

DESCRIPTION OF A MOTHER

A mother can be almost any size or any age, but she won't admit to anything over thirty. A mother has soft hands and smells good. A mother likes new dresses, music, a clean house, her children's kisses, an automatic washer....

A mother doesn't like having her children sick, muddy feet, temper tantrums, loud noise or bad report cards. A mother can read a thermometer...and, like magic, can kiss a hurt away.

A mother can bake good cakes and pies but likes to see her children eat vegetables. A mother can stuff a fat baby into a snowsuit in seconds and can kiss sad little faces and make them smile.

A mother is underpaid, has long hours and gets very little rest. She worries too much about her children, but she says she doesn't mind at all. And no matter how old her children are, she still likes to think of them as her little babies.

She is the guardian angel of the family, the queen, the tender hand of love. A mother is the best friend anyone ever has. A mother is love.

Author Unknown

YOUNG MOTHER

She holds him in her arms
  And murmurs lullabies;
While all the hope of motherhood
  Is shining in her eyes.

His eyes are pools that mirror
  Her dreams, her joys, her fears;
And in their depths is hidden
  The wonder of the years.

Kay Wissinger

Mother...in her eyes
the look of love....

Karen Ravn

MOTHERS ARE WONDERFUL

Mothers should know everything,
  Like just how high is "up,"
How to kiss away a hurt
  Or how to wash a pup;
Mothers should know everything,
  Like how to mend old toys,
And how to tell a story
  That delights small girls and boys;
Mothers should know everything,
  Like how to fly a kite,
What makes a budding flower bloom,
  Why stars come out at night;
Mothers should know everything,
  (Even why the sky is blue!)
Yes, mothers should know everything,
  And the wonder is — they DO!

Mary Dawson Hughes

BLESS MOTHERS EVERYWHERE

Bless mothers everywhere
    For being kind and sweet,
For teaching little hands to pray,
    For guiding little feet;
Bless them for their patience
    And understanding ways;
Bless them for their laughter
    And tender words of praise;
Bless them for the love they give
    That's constant, warm and true;
Bless them now and always
    In everything they do.

Katherine Plumb

A mother is not a person to lean on,
    but a person to make leaning unnecessary.

Dorothy Canfield Fisher

TENDERNESS

There is an enduring tenderness in the love of a mother to a son that transcends all other affections of the heart. It is neither to be chilled by selfishness, nor daunted by danger, nor weakened by worthlessness, nor stifled by ingratitude. She will sacrifice every comfort to his convenience; she will surrender every pleasure to his enjoyment; she will glory in his fame and exalt in his prosperity; and if adversity overtake him, he will be the dearer to her by misfortune; and if disgrace settle upon his name, she will still love and cherish him; and if all the world beside cast him off, she will be all the world to him.

Washington Irving

A MOTHER

In her the creative genius of God attains its highest skill. What a charming blend she is of the most lovable and moving qualities of human nature. From the moment in youth when she holds her first baby in her arms until in life's evening time she looks tenderly upon her grandchild, her life is one of dedicated service and love. Loving us, believing in us, fighting for us, praying for us, to her we are always her dear child — life of her life.

Norman Vincent Peale

HOME

Home to me is laughter,
   kisses on the cheek,
     warm looks and tender touches
   when the heart's too full
   to speak.
Home is sharing happiness
   and dreams I'm dreaming of —
Home to me is Mother,
Home to me is love.

Mary Loberg

M other is a gardener —
     planting the seeds of faith,
       truth and love that develop
   into the fairest flowers of character,
    virtue and happiness
       in the lives of her children.

J. Harold Gwynne

WHAT IS A MOTHER MADE OF?

A little wisdom
    to help her guide
    her children's steps
        while they're by her side,
A little strength
    to help erase
    whatever problems
        they might face...
That's what a mother is made of.

A little praise
    for a job well done,
    a little nonsense,
        a little fun,
A little warmth,
        a gentle touch
    that shows she cares
        so very much...
That's what a mother is made of.

A little trust
     from day to day
  as her children seek
     to find their way,
A little faith
     in the lives they lead
  and all the love
     her children need...
That's what a mother is made of.

Kay Andrew

A little praise
for a job well done…
That's what
a mother is made of.

Kay Andrew

LOVE

You see a mother's love
   in a table set with care,
a stack of mending
   by her favorite chair,
a room that's decorated
   with her own special flair —
These are the things love is made of.

You see it when she cooks
   her family's favorite dishes,
listens to each problem,
   the secret dreams and wishes,
when she tucks the children in
   with loving hugs and kisses —
These are the things love is made of.

Amy Cassidy

LIKE THE FOREST

What is a mother? Who shall answer this?
A mother is a font and spring of life,
A mother is a forest in whose heart
Lies hid a secret ancient as the hills,
For men to claim and take its wealth away;
And like the forest shall her wealth renew
And give, and give again, that men may live.

Francis Cardinal Spellman

Mothers' arms are made
of tenderness,
and sweet sleep blesses
the child who lies therein.

Victor Hugo

THE HEROISM OF THE MOTHER

Is not the highest heroism that which is free even from the approbation of the best and wisest? The heroism which is known only to our Father, who seeth in secret? The God-like lives lived in obscurity? How many thousands of heroines there must be now, of whom we shall never know. But still they are there. They sow in secret the seed of which we pluck the flower, and eat the fruit, and know not that we pass the sower daily in the streets.

One form of heroism — the most common, and yet the least remembered of all — namely, the heroism of the average mother. Ah! When I think of that broad fact, I gather hope again for poor humanity; and this dark world looks bright — this diseased world looks wholesome to me once more — because, whatever else it is not full of, it is at least full of mothers.

Charles Kingsley

M others…
think of the lessons of love
they taught to us!

Louis Conrad Hill

DEFINITION

I search among the plain and lovely words
To find what one word "Mother" means, as well
Try to define the tangled song of birds;
The echo in the hills of one clear bell.
One cannot snare the wind, or catch the wings
Of shadows flying low across the wheat;
Ah, who can prison simple, natural things
That make the long days beautiful and sweet?

Mother — a word that holds the tender spell
Of all the dear essential things of earth;
A home, clean sunlit rooms, and the good smell
Of bread; a table spread; a glowing hearth.
And love beyond the dream of anyone....
I search for words for her...and there are none.

Grace Noll Crowell

A MOTHER'S WORLD

A mother's world is a gentle world:
    a world of satin and sachet...
    of hugs and kisses
    and lullabies
       as soft as moonlight.

A mother's world is a busy world:
    a world of half-price sales and shopping carts...
    of school supplies and permanent press
    and learning math
       while cooking supper.

A mother's world is a happy world:
    a world of laughter and song...
    of family fun around the dinner table
    and love that reaches out
       and lasts forever.

Barbara Burrow

THE PICTURE

The painter has with his brush transferred the landscape to the canvas with such fidelity that the trees and grasses seem almost real; he has made even the face of a maiden seem instinct with life, but there is one picture so beautiful that no painter has ever been able perfectly to reproduce it, and that is the picture of the mother holding in her arms her babe.

William Jennings Bryan

The angels, whispering to one another,
    Can find, among their burning terms of love,
None so devotional as that of "Mother"....

Edgar Allan Poe

THE LITTLE THINGS

It is the little things that count
    And give a mother pleasure —
The things her children bring to her
    Which they so richly treasure...
The picture that is smudged a bit
    With tiny fingerprints,
The colored rock, the lightning bugs,
    The sticky peppermints,
The ragged, bright bouquet of flowers
    A child brings, roots and all —
These things delight a mother's heart,
    Although they seem quite small.
A mother can see beauty
    In the very smallest thing,
For there's a little bit of heaven
    In a small child's offering.

Theresa Ann Hunt

SHARING

A mother laughs our laughter,
    Sheds our tears,
Returns our love,
    Fears our fears.
She lives our joys,
    Cares our cares,
And all our hopes and dreams
      she shares.

Julia Summers

Beautiful, the earth around her —
    peaceful, the sky above,
Harmony and joy surround her —
    gentle is a mother's love.

Ed Cunningham

BECAUSE SHE IS A MOTHER

She broke the bread into two fragments and gave them to the children, who ate with avidity. "She hath kept none for herself," grumbled the Sergeant. "Because she is not hungry," said a soldier. "Because she is a mother," said the Sergeant.

Victor Hugo

Mother...
in her eyes
the look of loving,
in her smile
the warmth of caring,
in her hands
the touch of comfort,
in her heart
the gift of sharing.

Karen Ravn

A WONDERFUL OCCUPATION

A woman who runs her house well is both its queen and its subject. She is the one who makes work possible for her husband and children; she protects them from worries, feeds them and cares for them. She is Minister of Finance, and, thanks to her, the household budget is balanced. She is Minister of Fine Arts, and it is to her doing if the house or apartment has charm. She is Minister of Family Education and responsible for the boys' entry into school and college and the girls' cleverness and cultivation. A woman should be proud of her success in making her house into a perfect little world as the greatest statesman of his in organizing a nation's affairs.

André Maurois

I t is the little things
that count
And give a mother
pleasure....

Theresa Ann Hunt

I LOVE YOU

A mother says "I love you"
in so many ways:
with crisp, clean sheets
and warm mittens on winter mornings,
with decorated birthday cakes
and Christmas cookies
and eggs cooked
just the way you like them.
A mother says "I love you"
when she leaves the porchlight on for you
and picks up your clothes,
when she keeps your secrets,
feeds your pets
and tapes your homemade valentines
to the refrigerator door.
But most of all,
a mother says "I love you"
by filling a home
with warmth,
tenderness
and love.

Amy Cassidy

WHAT IS A MOTHER?

What is a mother? Two enterprising reporters, Joan Scobey and Lee Parr McGrath, decided to ask the experts — children. In their book What Is a Mother, *they report:*

A mother is the only one, if she sings your favorite song, it stops thundering.

Louise

Mothers are wonderful! She spends all her time on you. A mother is just like God, except God is better.

Laura

It is lucky that we have a mother because if we did not have a mother everything would be in a big big mess.

Fred

What is a mother? When I have something to tell somebody I can tell my mother sometimes but not all the times.

Betsy

A mother is a person too.

David

ONLY ONE MOTHER

Hundreds of stars in the pretty sky,
    Hundreds of shells on the shore together,
Hundreds of birds that go singing by,
    Hundreds of birds in the sunny weather.

Hundreds of dewdrops to greet the dawn,
    Hundreds of bees in the purple clover,
Hundreds of butterflies on the lawn,
    But only one mother the wide world over.

Author Unknown

Mother is a gardener —
    planting the seeds
of faith, truth and love....

J. Harold Gwynne

THE MOST BEAUTIFUL WORD

The most beautiful word in our language is Mother. Her tender hands wrought for us before we entered the world. Her weary feet never failed to carry her at night to see that we were safe in dreamland. In the long, dark hours she watched and prayed. She shared our sorrows and gave us our joys.

Author Unknown

Mothers...
Think of the shoes they tied for us,
The clothes they washed and dried for us,
The butter and jelly they spread for us,
The times they made the bed for us;
Think of the joys they brought to us
And the lessons of love they taught to us!

Louis Conrad Hill

WHY GOD MADE MOTHERS

God knew that everybody needs
    Someone to show the way,
He knew that babies need someone
    To care for them each day...
He knew they needed someone sweet
    To soothe their baby cries,
To teach them how to walk and talk
    And sing them lullabies...
That's why God made mothers.

He knew small children need someone
    To lend a guiding hand,
To answer all their questions
    And to smile and understand,
Someone to read them storybooks,
    To teach them wrong from right,
To show them wonderful new games
    And hear their prayers at night...
That's why God made mothers.

And then throughout their childhood years,
   God knew that children need
Someone to smile at them with pride,
   Encourage each new deed.
As they grow up and all their lives,
   God knew that everywhere,
All children need a mother's heart
   To understand and care,
And that's why God made mothers.

Katherine Nelson Davis

A mother is the only person on earth
   who can divide her love among ten children
and each child still have all her love.

Author Unknown

A mother is
all those wonderful things
you never outgrow
your need for.

Kay Andrew

A MOTHER'S HEART

The door that leads to a mother's heart
   Is always open wide,
And in her heart is a special place
   Where peace and love abide.
There is no lock on a mother's heart,
   Her children freely go
For a pat on the cheek or a comforting word
   Or something they want to know.
Through years of work and prayer she's learned
   Her wise and tender art,
For the nearest thing to the love of God
   Is the love of a mother's heart.

Barbara Burrow

Body copy is set in Goudy Old Style, a roman typeface designed by F. W. Goudy c. 1915. Display type is Parisian, a modified sans serif created by M. F. Benton for American Type-founders in 1928. Printed on Hallmark Crown Royale Book paper.
Designed by Leanne Mishler.